P9-DCR-720

ANIMAL
Tongues

Cataloging Information

Cusick, Dawn.
    Animal tongues/Dawn Cusick
        36 p. : col. ill. ; 20 cm.
    Includes index (p.).
    Summary: Explores the morphology and behavior of animal tongues.
        Includes a range of taxa, including mammals, insects, birds,
        reptiles, fish, and mollusks.
    LC: QL 946
    Dewey: 591.4
    ISBN-13: 978-0-9797455-1-5 (alk. paper)
    ISBN-10:   0-9797455-1-9 (alk. paper)
        Tongue—Juvenile literature

Art Director: Susan McBride
Page Layout: Beth Fielding
Photo Research: Beth Fielding
Copy Editor: Susan Brill

10 9 8 7 6 5 4 3 2 1

First edition

Published by EarlyLight Books, Inc.
1436 Dellwood Road
Waynesville, NC 28786

To Will & Wes

ANIMAL
Tongues

Dawn Cusick

EarlyLight Books

WAYNESVILLE, NORTH CAROLINA, USA

STICKY TONGUES
WARMING TONGUES
TALKING TONGUES
TASTING TONGUES

TRICK TONGUES
COOLING TONGUES
CLEANING TONGUES
SHORT TONGUES

COLORFUL TONGUES
SMELLING TONGUES
CURLY TONGUES
THIN TONGUES

TUBE TONGUES
FORK TONGUES
GLOW-IN-THE-DARK TONGUES
THICK TONGUES
LONG TONGUES

TEST IT OUT: Try saying the following classic tongue twister without moving your tongue at all. Peter Piper picked a peck of pickled peppers. What happens? Can your friend understand a single word you're saying? How hard do you have to concentrate to keep your tongue from moving?

PEOPLE Tongues

People use their tongues to help taste, chew, and swallow food the same way many other animals do. We also use our tongues for something pretty amazing: to talk! Words are formed by moving air through our mouths in special ways, and our tongues help shape the way the air moves and sounds.

Human tongues are covered with about 10,000 taste buds when we're young, and only half as many when we're adults. Taste buds help us know when something is sweet, salty, sour, or bitter.

Ever wonder why most people have bad breath when they first wake up in the morning? Bacteria caught between the taste buds (remember how many there are!) make a stinky smell.

DOG Tongues

D ogs would die if they didn't have tongues! When people get hot, we lower our body temperature by sweating through sweat glands.

Dogs only have sweat glands on the bottoms of their paws, so they lower their body temperatures with their tongues! When a dog sticks out its tongue and pants, it cools its mouth and tongue, and also the blood circulating in its head.

Dogs also hang their tongues out when they are looking forward to a special treat or something they love to do, like going for a walk.

GUESS WHAT? Full-bred chow and shar-pei dogs have blue-black tongues, and the reason is a mystery! Sometimes other breeds of dogs have small blue-black spots on their tongues. No one knows why that is, either.

CAT Tongues

All kinds of cats — little cats, big cats, house cats, wild cats — use their tongues to clean their fur. A cat's tongue has lots of small bumps on it (called papillae), and each bump has a small hook at the end of it.

Papillae hooks act like combs when a cat licks itself, removing loose fur, dirt, and food particles from the cat's fur. Papillae hooks are too small to see without a microscope, but they are why your cat's tongue feels so rough when it licks your skin.

Tongue baths do more for cats than keep them clean. When it's hot outside, a tongue bath helps cool them off, and when it's cold, a tongue bath smoothes the fur hairs close together so the cat's body heat stays next to its skin.

Tongue baths also help cats spread scent molecules in their saliva onto their fur so mommy cats can recognize their kittens and cubs.

GIRAFFE
Tongues

Giraffes use their long (almost 2 feet long!) tongues to pull the tops of tall tree branches down to their mouths so they can eat the leaves. Their tongues are so strong that giraffes can pull down heavy branches and chew thorns without hurting themselves. Scientists describe the giraffe's tongue as prehensile, which means it has adapted for holding and grasping.

People are often amazed when they see a giraffe's tongue up close because it's black. Since giraffes need to eat leaves all day to get enough food, their tongues are exposed to a lot of sun. Scientists believe the black tongue color keeps it from getting sunburned!

TEST IT OUT: Pretend you're trying to clean some cake frosting off the side of your mouth with your tongue. Can you feel your tongue stretching? Now imagine you have cake frosting stuck in your ear. Can you stretch your tongue that far? Giraffes use their tongues to clean bugs out of their ears. Wonder if they'd like some cake frosting?

NECTAR BAT Tongues

A nectar bat from South America takes the prize for the longest tongue: it's 1.5 times longer than its body!

Scientists believe the bat has such a long tongue because it feeds on the nectar of a very long flower. The bat's tongue is a hollow tube, like a soda straw, so that it can suck the nectar from inside the flower. Where does the bat keep its long tongue when it's not eating? In its rib cage, of course!

The nectar bat shown here is from southeastern Arizona, and its favorite food is the sweet nectar in flowering cactus.

TEST IT OUT: To see how long the nectar bat's tongue is, stand against a wall and have a friend measure your height. Multiply the measurement by 1.5. Cut a piece of yarn or string to this length, then hold it against one side of your mouth and imagine how you would fit a tongue this long into your mouth.

SNAKE Tongues

eople who don't like snakes really don't like snake tongues. When they see the snake's tongue flicking in and out, they often get scared or grossed out. The snake isn't trying to scare them, though, it's just trying to smell them.

When a snake flicks its tongue in and out, the tip of the snake's tongue collects scent molecules from the air and brings them back to the Jacobson organ on the roof of its mouth. The Jacobson's organ tells the snake if there's a tasty snack (a big fat rat, maybe?) nearby. The V shape (also called a fork) in the snake's tongue helps tell the snake which direction a smell is coming from. Male snakes also use their tongues to smell the air for females.

TOTALLY COOL: **Snakes don't have to open their mouths to stick out their tongue. Instead, the tongue goes through a hole on the top of the mouth.**

BET YOU DIDN'T KNOW . . . When a
snake sheds the skin on its body, it also sheds
the skin on its tongue!!!

17

TEST IT OUT: Suck on a blue popsicle until your tongue is bright blue, then go stick your tongue out at your Mom and see if she's afraid or surprised!

BLUE-TONGUE SKINK
Tongues

B lue-tongue skinks are one of six different types of Australian lizards that have blue tongues. They use their tongues to smell their surroundings in the same way snakes do. They also use their tongues to scare away predators such as eagles, snakes, and large lizards that are trying to eat them!

When a predator comes too close, the blue-tongue skink first tries to make it go away by hissing and making its body look big. If that doesn't work, the skink sticks out its long, blue tongue.

Some scientists think the sudden appearance of a bright blue tongue surprises predators, giving the skink a chance to run away to safety. Other scientists think the bright blue tongue works like a warning color, telling predators that the skink is poisonous and might bite.

CHAMELEON
Tongues

A chameleon's best hunting tool is its amazing trick tongue. The tongue shoots out of the chameleon's mouth with force from a very strong muscle. As the tongue comes out, it stretches up to six times its length. In fact, a chameleon's stretched-out tongue can be as long as one and a half times longer than its body!

Now imagine the chameleon is hiding in a bush, waiting for a tasty insect to fly nearby. Its tongue is fast and long, but how does it catch breakfast? When the tip of a chameleon's tongue hits its target, the edges fold around the prey, holding it tight until the tasty treat is back in its mouth.

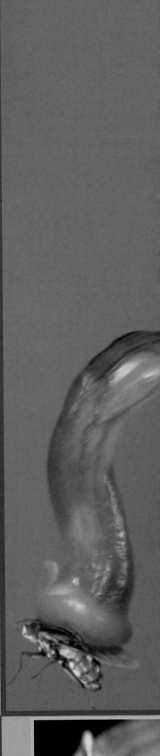

HOW FAST IS FAST? Want to know how fast a chameleon's tongue comes out of its mouth? Clap your hands together once or snap your fingers. In the time your hands were together, a chemeleon's tongue could have shot out of its mouth 16 different times!!!

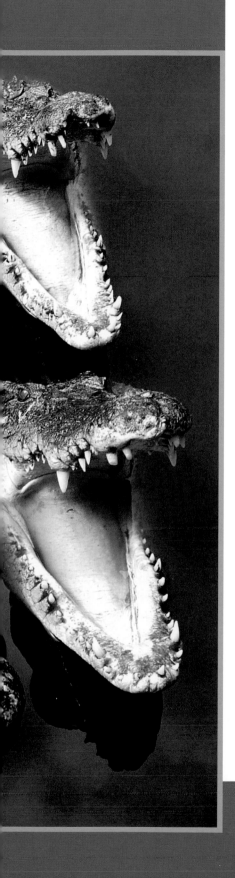

CROCODILE Tongues

Did you try the **Test It Out** challenge on page 6 that asks you to say a tongue twister without moving your tongue? If a crocodile tried to say the same tongue twister, its words wouldn't make any sense either. Crocodile tongues are attached to the bottom of their mouths and can't move. Because their tongues can't move, they can't use them to help chew their food. Instead, crocodiles have extra-strong digestive acids that start breaking their food in pieces before they swallow. It's a good thing crocodiles only talk in cartoons!

Crocodile tongues have special glands that let them live in salt water. Salt that builds up in the crocodile's body is squeezed out through the salt glands so the extra salt can't hurt their bodies. Alligators do not have salt glands on their tongues and would die in a few days if they tried to live in salt water.

KILLER WHALE
Tongues

Killer whales, also called orcas, have bright pink tongues. Because they are mammals, newborn whale calves drink milk from their mothers when they're young. When a human baby nurses, its mom sits down and holds it.

Whale moms, though, have to keep swimming while they nurse, and they don't have arms to hold on to the babies. Instead, baby whales have small bumps (papillae) on the edges of their tongues that help them hang on tight to their moms while they're nursing.

Orcas were named "killer whales" in the 1800s by fishermen who watched the orcas attack and kill large baleen whales. The fishermen saw the orcas biting at the mouths of the baleen whales, eating just their lips and tongues!

BABY DOLPHINS also have papillae bumps on their tongues to help them nurse and hang on while mom swims.

GUESS WHAT? Scientists have found that the baleen whale's tongue helps move heat through the whale's body while it hunts for food with its mouth open in cold ocean water. The tongue works like a built-in heater!

TONGUE SHAPES TELL STORIES! You can usually tell what a bird eats by the shape of its tongue. Birds that suck nectar have hollow, straw-like tongues, while birds that scoop nectar out of flowers have brush-like shapes at the tips of their tongues. Birds that use their tongues to catch bugs, such as woodpeckers, have pointed, spear-like tongues or sticky tongues. And birds that eat a lot of slippery fish have pointy spikes on their tongues that help push the fish down their throats!

PARROT Tongues

Most birds use their tongues to get food. Parrots eat a lot of big seeds, and their strong tongues help them hold and crush the seed shells.

Many parrots also use their tongue to help them make sounds and say words. The sounds are formed in the back of the birds' throat, then the birds move their tongues back and forth while they talk, which changes the shape of the air and the sounds they produce.

HUMMINGBIRD MOTH
Tongues

Like many butterflies, hummingbird moths get their food by sucking sweet nectar through their tongues (called a proboscis) from flowers. Their tongues are hollow, like drinking straws, and thin, like a sewing needle.

Since hummingbird moths sometimes need to get nectar from very big flowers, they need very long tongues. Their tongues are often longer than their bodies . . . wait—stop for a minute and think about that . . . imagine your tongue is as long as your body . . . how would you fit it in your mouth? The hummingbird moth keeps its long tongue coiled up in a tight circle under its head when it's not being used.

WHAT'S IN A NAME? Hummingbird moths were named after hummingbirds because both have wings that make a humming sound when they hover near a flower. Hummingbird moths share another trait with hummingbirds: a very long tongue! A hummingbird's tongue is too long to fit in its mouth so some of the tongue stays in the front of the bird's head, in its skull!

ABOVE: A curled-up tongue

RIGHT: An extended tongue drawing nectar from a flower

Tongue Trivia

LIZARDFISH MAY LOOK SWEET AND PRETTY, BUT THEIR TONGUES are lined with teeth on both sides! Lizardfish use these extra teeth to help them hang on to the small fish they catch for dinner!

SUPPOSE SOMEONE SAID YOU COULD HAVE AS MANY CANDY BARS AS YOU COULD FIT IN YOUR MOUTH. How many candy bars could you eat? Atlantic puffin birds live near oceans and love fish more than some people love candy bars. To hold lots of fish in their beaks, puffin birds use their tongues to press each fish against sharp spines on the inside of their mouths. While their tongues hold the newly caught fish, their beaks can open wide and catch more fish!

Tongue Trivia

GARDEN SNAIL TONGUES have curly edges, like ribbon, and are covered in horn-like teeth. The snail scrapes its sharp teeth over the ground to pull lichen and algae off the ground. Yummm, tasty!

WHEN DOES A HOUSEFLY'S TONGUE COME OUT? Flies have nerve cells on the bottoms of their feet that know when they've landed on something sweet. The nerve cells send a message to the fly's brain: "Stick out your tongue." Out comes the fly's proboscis, a long, hollow tongue that lets the fly suck food through its tongue like a soda straw.

BLOWING RASPBERRIES . . . When polar bears stick out their tongues, zoo visitors are usually surprised to see their tongues are black and blue! Scientists don't know why polar bear tongues aren't solid pink, like those of many other types of bears, but it may be to protect them from sunburn.

Tongue Trivia

WORST BREATH ON EARTH: Which animal has a yellow tongue and very bad breath? The largest lizard in the world, the komodo dragon. Komodo dragons use their long, forked tongues the same way snakes do, to smell the air around them for tasty prey. Who says dragons only exist in fairy tales?

OUCH! TONGUE PARASITES LOOK PAINFUL! These parasites are called tongue-eating louse. A louse bites into a red snapper's tongue and lives there, sucking the snapper's blood. Don't feel too bad for the snapper, though; the fish can still use its tongue!

Tongue Trivia

GLOW-IN-THE-DARK FUNG-TONGUES . . . What on earth, you ask, is a fung-tongue? The tuatara fung-tongue is a close relative of snakes and lizards that live in caves in New Zealand. A special kind of glow-in-the-dark fungus grows on the end of the fung-tongue's tongue. When the fung-tongue wants to catch some insects for food, it holds its mouth wide open. Insects are attracted to the light from the fungus and fly into the fung-tongue's mouth!

NUDIBRANCHS, A TYPE OF OCEAN SEA SLUG, eat their favorite dinner from the inside out! To eat a sea squirt, the nudibranch puts its tongue into the opening of a sea squirt, and sucks out the tender meat inside.

NUDIBRANCH

SEA SQUIRT

NUDIBRANCH USING ITS TONGUE TO EAT A SEA SQUIRT FROM THE INSIDE OUT

Glossary

PAPILLAE: Papillae are small protrusions on tongues. They come in different shapes and help animals in different ways. For cats, the hook-shaped papillae help them remove dirt and loose fur from their coats. For aquatic mammals such as dolphins and whales, papillae bumps help newborns hold on tight to their moms while nursing. In humans, taste buds sit on the tops of papillae.

PREHENSILE: Prehensile describes the adapted ability of a body part on an animal to grasp or hold an object, usually by wrapping the body part around the object. Common prehensile body parts are tails, tongues, and toes.

PROBOSCIS: A proboscis is a thin, tube-like, sucking and feeding organ found in worms, bugs, and mollusks. When people see a proboscis come out of a worm, insect, or mollusk mouth, they usually call it a tongue.

TASTE BUD: Taste buds are sensory organs that sit on the top of papillae. They have very small hairs that send chemical messages to the brain. The messages tell whether something is sweet, sour, salty, or bitter.

LEFT: Close-up of hook-shaped papillae on a housecat's tongue
RIGHT: Close-up of taste buds on a cow's tongue

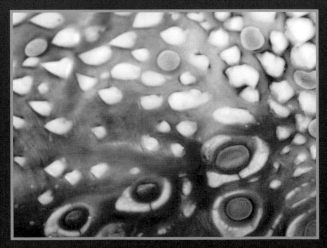

ACKNOWLEDGMENTS

Research by the following biologists contributed many of the fascinating facts in this book: Gabriel Beckers, Daniel Bensen, Pier F. Ferrari, Anthony Herrel, John E. Heyning, Shin-ichi Iwasaki, Jim Mead, Jay Meyers, Nathan Muchhala, Ulrike Müller, David Namen, Brian Nelson, Stephen Suomi, Roderick Suthers, and Inga de Vries.

PHOTO CREDITS

Charles W. Melton (bat photos, pages 14 and 15)
Leanne & David Atkinson (tongue parasite photo, page 32)
Leanne & David Atkinson (feeding nudibranch photo, page 33)

CLOCKWISE FROM TOP RIGHT: A bear, an eagle, a snow leopard, a rainbow lizard, and a butterfly show off their tongues.

Index

The End!